RAMA
ON THE BANK OF THE RIVER SARAYU STANDS THE CITY OF AYODHYA. LONG AGO, RAJA DASHARATHA RULED OVER IT. HE HAD FOUR SONS-RAMA, LAXMANA, BHARATA AND SHATRUGHNA.

RAMA WAS BORN OF QUEEN KAUSHALYA, BHARATA OF QUEEN KAIKEYI AND LAXMANA AND SHATRUGHNA OF QUEEN SUMITRA. BUT THEY WERE ALL DEEPLY ATTACHED TO ONE ANOTHER.

RAMA'S SKILL WITH THE BOW AND ARROW WAS KNOWN FAR AND WIDE. IN THE JUNGLE, SAGE VISHWAMITRA ALSO REMEMBERED IT.

SO, WITH THE PERMISSION OF KING DASHARATHA, RAMA AND LAXMANA WERE BROUGHT TO THE JUNGLE. ONE DAY–
RAMA! HERE COMES THE DEMONESS TATAKA.
THERE WAS A FIERCE BATTLE BETWEEN TATAKA AND RAMA.
AND FINALLY–
THERE WERE MORE RAIDS BY DEMONS. BUT RAMA'S ARROWS NEVER MISSED THEIR MARK.

THE ANIMALS AND BIRDS ROAM ABOUT FREELY NOW.
YES, THE DEMONS BOTHER THEM NO MORE, MY SON!

A FEW DAYS LATER –
WE SHALL GO TO WITNESS THE SWAYAMVARA OF SITA, THE DAUGHTER OF RAJA JANAKA.

IN KING JANAKA'S PALACE –
HE WHO SUCCEEDS IN STRINGING THE BOW WILL WIN SITA'S HAND IN MARRIAGE.

ONE AFTER ANOTHER, PRINCES TRIED TO STRING THE BOW. THEY COULD NOT EVEN LIFT IT.
EACH ONE OF US HAS FAILED. SURELY WE CAN LIFT THIS BOW TOGETHER!
RAMA, MY SON! ALL THE OTHERS HAVE FAILED. NOW LIFT THE BOW AND BRING HAPPINESS TO SITA!
RAMA LIFTED THE BOW EASILY. IT BROKE UNDER HIS STRENGTH.
SITA LOOKED UP AND WAS PLEASED TO SEE RAMA.

WHEN THE HAPPY NEWS REACHED AYODHYA, KING DASHARATHA LEFT FOR MITHILA, AT THE HEAD OF A PROCESSION..

... WHERE RAMA WAS MARRIED TO SITA.

OH! I AM GETTING TOO OLD! IT IS TIME TO HAND OVER THE KINGDOM TO RAMA.
YEARS PASSED BY HAPPILY. ONE DAY —
ALL WERE PLEASED TO HEAR THE NEWS — EXCEPT MANTHARA, QUEEN KAIKEYI'S MAID.
RAMA WILL BE CROWNED SOON!
NOT IF I CAN HELP IT!
WHAT'S WRONG MANTHARA?
RAMA IS TO BE CROWNED KING TOMORROW. YOUR SON, BHARATA, HAS NOT EVEN BEEN SENT FOR FROM HIS MATERNAL UNCLE'S HOME.

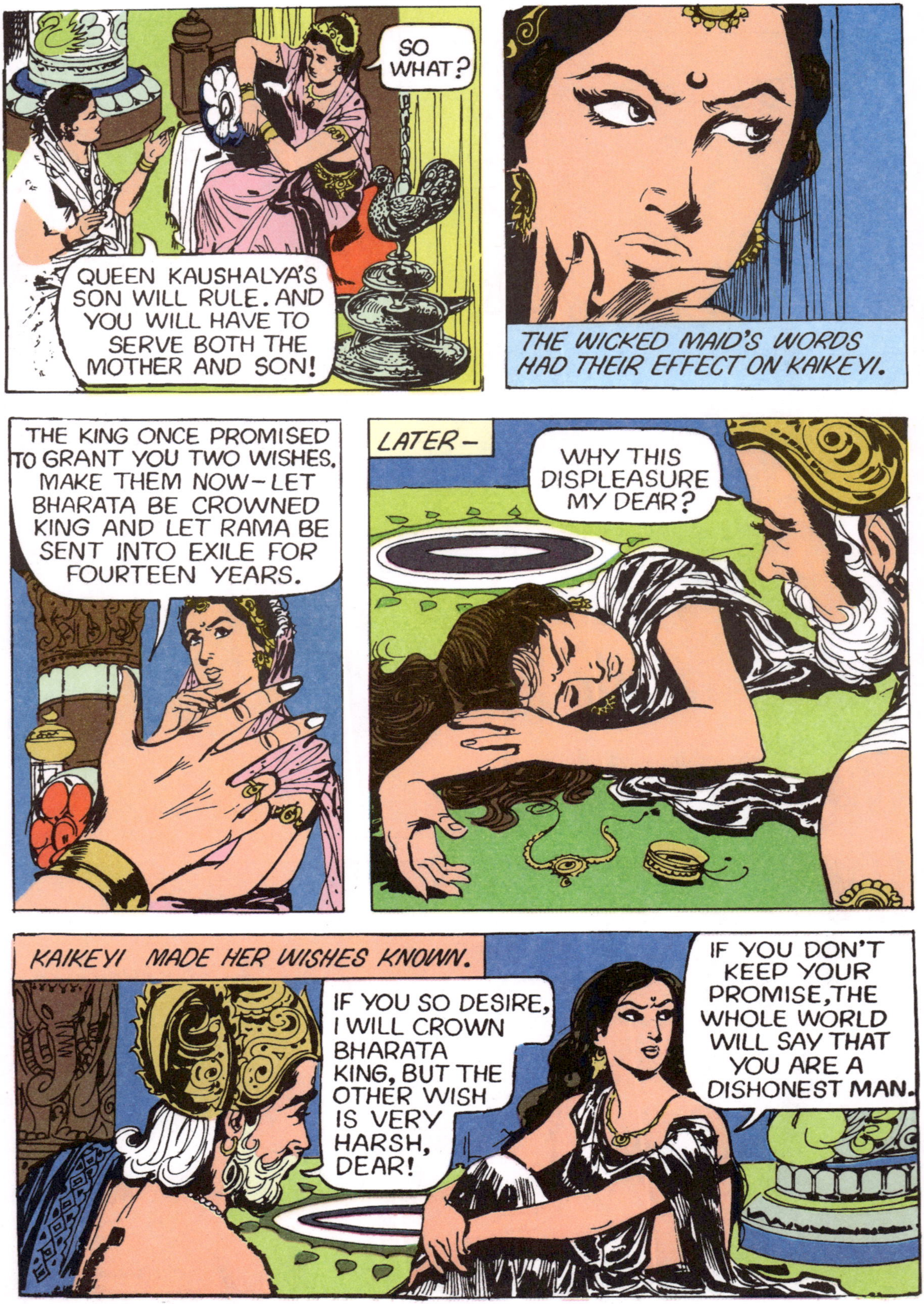
SO WHAT?
QUEEN KAUSHALYA'S SON WILL RULE. AND YOU WILL HAVE TO SERVE BOTH THE MOTHER AND SON!
THE WICKED MAID'S WORDS HAD THEIR EFFECT ON KAIKEYI.
THE KING ONCE PROMISED TO GRANT YOU TWO WISHES. MAKE THEM NOW – LET BHARATA BE CROWNED KING AND LET RAMA BE SENT INTO EXILE FOR FOURTEEN YEARS.
LATER –
WHY THIS DISPLEASURE MY DEAR?
KAIKEYI MADE HER WISHES KNOWN.
IF YOU SO DESIRE, I WILL CROWN BHARATA KING, BUT THE OTHER WISH IS VERY HARSH, DEAR!
IF YOU DON'T KEEP YOUR PROMISE, THE WHOLE WORLD WILL SAY THAT YOU ARE A DISHONEST MAN.

THE KING FELL DOWN ON THE GROUND WHEN HE HEARD THESE HARSH WORDS.
HOW COULD YOU BE SO CRUEL TO RAMA? HE IS SO GOOD AND NOBLE.
WHEN RAMA LEARNT OF IT –
I SHALL KEEP MY FATHER'S PROMISE, MOTHER!
SITA AND LAXMANA ALSO INSISTED ON ACCOMPANYING RAMA TO THE JUNGLES. THE PEOPLE OF AYODHYA ALSO FOLLOWED THEM.
MINISTER, SIR, COULDN'T YOU PERSUADE THESE PEOPLE TO GO BACK?
WE SHALL ALL COME WITH YOU.
WHEN DUSK FELL, THEY STOPPED AND RESTED. EARLY NEXT MORNING–
LET US BE GONE BEFORE THE PEOPLE WAKE UP AND INSIST ON GOING WITH US.

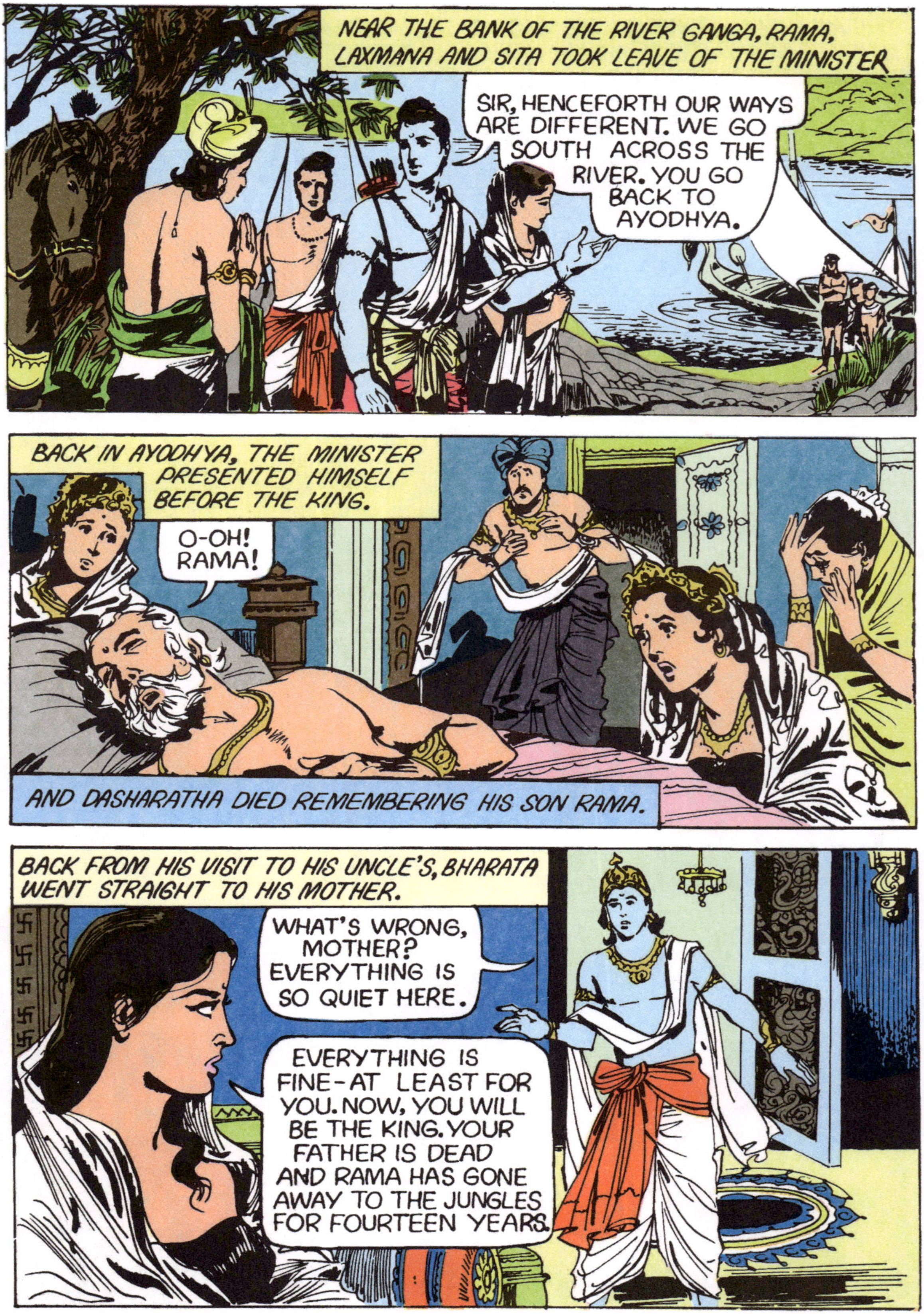
NEAR THE BANK OF THE RIVER GANGA, RAMA, LAXMANA AND SITA TOOK LEAVE OF THE MINISTER
SIR, HENCEFORTH OUR WAYS ARE DIFFERENT. WE GO SOUTH ACROSS THE RIVER. YOU GO BACK TO AYODHYA.
BACK IN AYODHYA, THE MINISTER PRESENTED HIMSELF BEFORE THE KING.
O-OH! RAMA!
AND DASHARATHA DIED REMEMBERING HIS SON RAMA.
BACK FROM HIS VISIT TO HIS UNCLE'S, BHARATA WENT STRAIGHT TO HIS MOTHER.
WHAT'S WRONG, MOTHER? EVERYTHING IS SO QUIET HERE.
EVERYTHING IS FINE-AT LEAST FOR YOU. NOW, YOU WILL BE THE KING. YOUR FATHER IS DEAD AND RAMA HAS GONE AWAY TO THE JUNGLES FOR FOURTEEN YEARS.

BHARATA WAS SHOCKED TO HEAR THE DETAILS. VASISHTHA, THE ROYAL PRIEST, TRIED TO CONSOLE HIM.
I DON'T WANT THE KINGDOM. I MUST GO TO RAMA AT ONCE.
FORGET YOUR SORROW! ATTEND TO THE MATTERS OF STATE! THAT IS YOUR DUTY!

AT CHITRAKOOT, WHERE RAMA, LAXMANA AND SITA HAD MADE THEIR HOME–
BHARATA IS MARCHING HIS ARMIES AGAINST US. I WILL...
LAXMANA, DON'T BE SO HASTY. LET THEM COME!

BHARATA, MY DEAR BROTHER!
DEAR RAMA! WE ALL WANT YOU TO GO BACK TO AYODHYA!
FORGIVE ME GURUDEV, I CAN'T BREAK MY FATHER'S PROMISE.
AND I CAN NOT ACCEPT THE KINGDOM. IF YOU ARE NOT COMING BACK, I SHALL RULE IN YOUR NAME. YOUR SANDALS WILL REPRESENT YOU.
AFTER BHARATA LEFT, RAMA, LAXMANA AND SITA SETTLED DOWN IN PANCHAVATI TOWN IN THE SOUTH. ONE DAY —
A HANDSOME MAN! AND POWERFUL TOO! I MUST WIN HIS LOVE.

NOBLE SIR, SHOORPANAKHA IS MY NAME. I OFFER MY LOVE; DO ACCEPT IT.
I AM A HAPPILY MARRIED MAN, LADY! YOU COULD ASK LAXMANA!
I AM ONLY HIS SERVANT! HE IS THE ONE FOR YOU.
SHOORPANAKHA ASSUMED A FRIGHTENING FORM AND RUSHED TOWARDS SITA.
ENRAGED, LAXMANA CHOPPED OFF HER NOSE AND EARS. SHE RAN TO HER COUSINS, KHARA AND DOOSHANA, FOR HELP.
OH-OH! KHAR! DOOSHAN!

KHAR! DOOSHAN! THEY DARED TO DO THIS TO YOUR SISTER!
WE WILL FIGHT THEM, SISTER!
KHARA AND DOOSHANA CAME WITH A MIGHTY ARMY OF DEMONS TO FIGHT RAMA.
THEY HAVE KILLED BOTH KHARA AND DOOSHANA! RUN FOR YOUR LIVES!
THE TEN-HEADED RAVANA, THE KING OF LANKA, WAS THE BROTHER OF SHOORPANAKHA. SHE NOW APPROACHED HIM.
YOU WILL BE AVENGED, MY SISTER! FIRST LET ME CONSULT UNCLE MAREECHA!

RAVANA APPROACHED MAREECHA.
RAVANA! RAMA IS POWERFUL. TO FIGHT HIM IS NOT EASY.
YOU ASSUME THE FORM OF A GOLDEN DEER AND LURE RAMA AWAY. MEAN-WHILE I WILL RUN AWAY WITH SITA.

IN PANCHAVATI -
THAT DEER IS SO BEAUTIFUL! I WANT IT.
I WILL GET IT FOR YOU, SITA.

RAMA CHASED THE DEER DEEP INTO THE JUNGLE - THE DEER CRIED OUT LOUDLY IN A HUMAN VOICE.
OH! LAXMANA!

RAMA IS CALLING YOU, LAXMANA.
BUT RAMA HAS ASKED ME NOT TO LEAVE YOU ALONE.
YOU MUST GO TO HELP YOUR BROTHER. LAXMANA.
I DIDN'T CALL YOU, LAXMANA! IT WAS A TRICK PLAYED BY THIS DEMON.
MEANWHILE, DISGUISED AS A SANYASI, RAVANA APPROACHED SITA.
WILL THE KIND LADY OFFER ME SOME FOOD?

AS SITA BROUGHT HIM FOOD, RAVANA CAUGHT HOLD OF HER...
...AND CARRIED HER AWAY IN HIS CHARIOT.
HELP! RAMA! LAXMANA! HELP!
SOMEONE SAVE ME FROM THIS DEVIL! PLEASE!
JATAYU, THE VULTURE, CAME TO HER HELP.
YOU OLD FOOL! YOU DARED TO FIGHT RAVANA!

WHEN RAMA REACHED THE SPOT IN SEARCH OF SITA -
I FAILED TO RESCUE SITA. RAVANA HAS TAKEN HER TO THE SOUTH.
POOR JATAYU HE GAVE HIS LIFE FOR ME!
TRAVELLING FURTHER SOUTH, RAMA MET SUGREEVA, BROTHER OF THE MONKEY KING VALI AND HIS MINISTER HANUMAN.
I AM ALSO SAD, RAMA. I LIVE IN THE JUNGLE FOR FEAR OF VALI, MY BROTHER, WHO HAS KID-NAPPED MY WIFE. HELP ME TO OVERTHROW VALI AND I WILL HELP YOU.
RAMA KILLED VALI AND SET SUGREEVA ON THE THRONE. VALI'S SON, ANGADA. WAS CROWNED PRINCE.
LATER—
NOW HANUMAN! YOU MUST GO IN SEARCH OF SITA.
HERE, HANUMAN! TAKE THIS RING. IF YOU FIND SITA, SHE WILL RECOGNISE THIS.

WANDERING FOR DAYS AND WEEKS, THE ARMY OF MONKEYS AND BEARS, LED BY PRINCE ANGADA, ATLAST REACHED THE SOUTHERN SEA COAST.
NOW, YOU ALONE CAN JUMP ACROSS THE SEA, HANUMAN!
HANUMAN LEAPED INTO THE SKY.
IN LANKA –
NOW TO LOOK FOR SITA!
ATLAST, IN A GARDEN –
THERE. THAT MUST BE SITA.

HANUMAN DROPPED RAMA'S RING.
I CAN'T LIVE WITHOUT RAMA. I WOULD RATHER KILL MYSELF... RAMA'S RING! HOW DID IT GET HERE!
I BROUGHT THIS RING WITH ME. I WILL TELL HIM YOU ARE HERE AND HE WILL SURELY COME AND KILL RAVANA!
HANUMAN JUMPED DOWN.
BUT BEFORE I GO, I MUST TEACH THESE DEMONS A LESSON.
IT IS THAT MONKEY! GET HIM! GET HIM!

HANUMAN HAD KNOCKED DOWN THE DEMONS IN AND AROUND THE GARDEN. RAVANA SENT MORE MEN WITH HIS SON, AKSHAYA KUMAR.

IN RAVANA'S COURT–
THAT MONKEY HAS KILLED PRINCE AKSHAY KUMAR AS WELL!
NOW, MEGHNAD, MY SON, ARREST THAT MONKEY AND BRING HIM HERE!

MEGHNAD CAPTURED HANUMAN AND BROUGHT HIM TO THE COURT.
SET FIRE TO THIS EVIL MONKEY'S TAIL.

THIS WILL BE FUN TO WATCH.

HANUMAN LOOSENED THE ROPES THAT BOUND HIM. HIS TAIL GREW BIGGER AND BIGGER. WITH HIS LONG TAIL AFIRE, HE SET FIRE TO THE WHOLE OF LANKA.
RUN! RUN FOR YOUR LIVES! THIS MONKEY IS DANGEROUS.

HAVING BURNT LANKA, HANUMAN RETURNED TO RAMA'S CAMP.
SITA IS IN LANKA. SHE ASKED ME TO GIVE YOU THIS JEWEL. LANKA SHOULD NOW BE INVADED!

WITH A HUGE ARMY OF MONKEYS, BEARS AND OTHERS, RAMA, LAXMANA, SUGREEVA AND HANUMAN ARRIVED ON THE COAST.

WHEN THE NEWS REACHED THE COURT OF RAVANA, HIS BROTHER, VIBHEESHANA GAVE HIM GOOD ADVICE.
ABDUCTING ANOTHER MAN'S WIFE IS NEITHER FAIR NOR WISE!

GET OUT OF HERE, VIBHEESHANA. GO, TEACH YOUR WISDOM TO THOSE BEGGARS!

NOBLE RAMA GAVE REFUGE TO VIBHEESHANA.
THE ENEMY'S BROTHER - IN OUR CAMP? I DON'T LIKE THE IDEA!
HE SEEKS ASYLUM, SUGREEVA! I CAN'T TURN HIM AWAY.
A BRIDGE WAS LAID ACROSS THE SEA.
TO LANKA
TO LANKA
TO LANKA
THE ARMIES WERE READY FOR THE BATTLE.
ANGADA, BEFORE WE GIVE THE CALL FOR BATTLE, PLEASE GO TO RAVANA'S COURT WITH A MESSAGE.

PRINCE ANGADA CAME TO THE COURT OF RAVANA.
RETURN SITA WITH HONOUR. LORD RAMA WILL MAKE PEACE WITH YOU.
GO, TELL RAMA THAT I WILL NOT SURRENDER! WE WANT WAR!

ANGADA RETURNED AND THE BATTLE CALL WAS GIVEN.

BRAVE LAXMANA FELL IN THE BATTLE, HIT WITH AN ARROW BY MEGHNAD, RAVANA'S SON.

IF ONLY THE PHYSICIAN SUSHENA COULD BE BROUGHT HERE...
I WILL BRING HIM!

HANUMAN BROUGHT SUSHENA ALONG WITH HIS HOUSE.

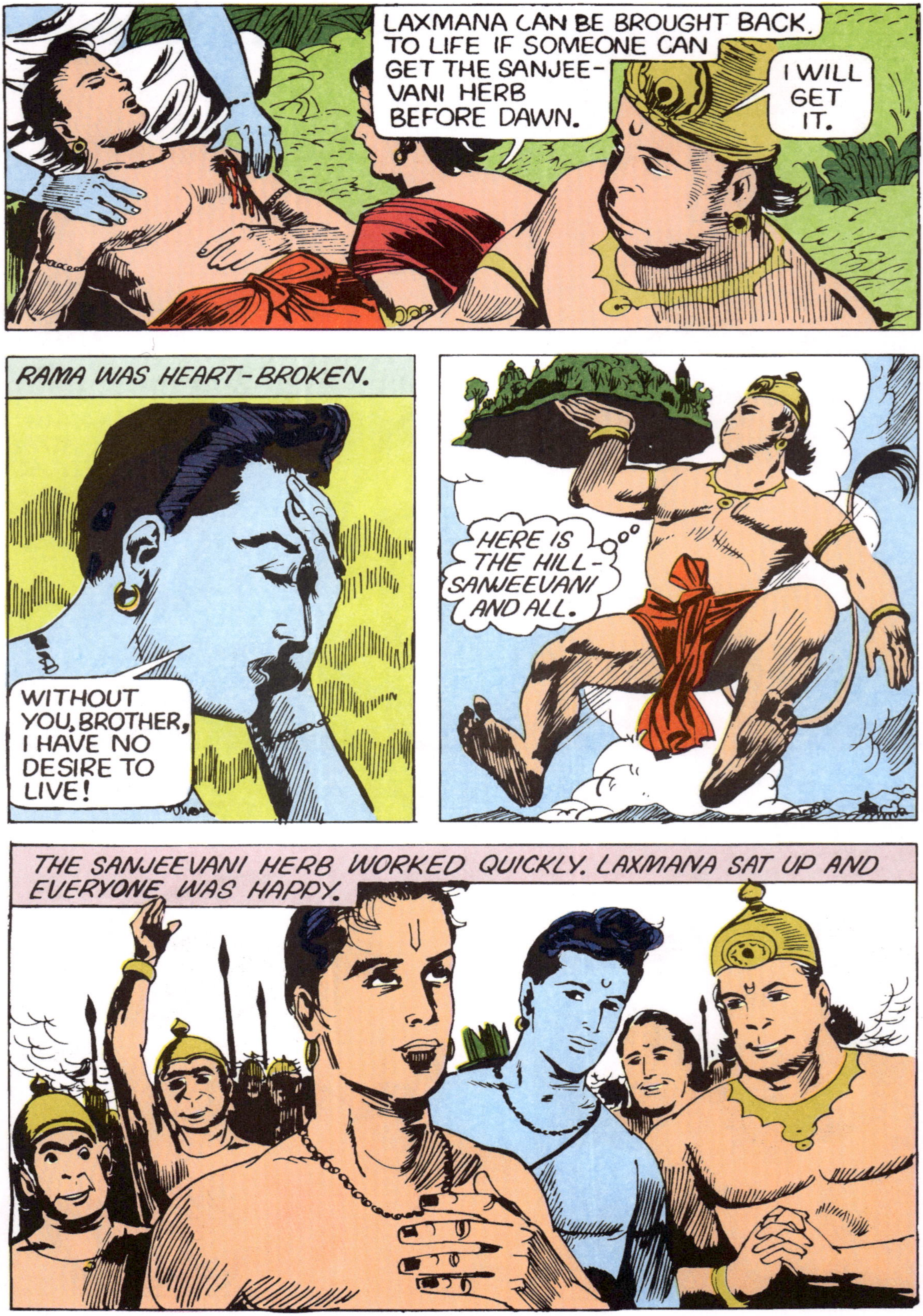
LAXMANA CAN BE BROUGHT BACK TO LIFE IF SOMEONE CAN GET THE SANJEE-VANI HERB BEFORE DAWN.
I WILL GET IT.
RAMA WAS HEART-BROKEN.
WITHOUT YOU, BROTHER, I HAVE NO DESIRE TO LIVE!
HERE IS THE HILL-SANJEEVANI AND ALL.
THE SANJEEVANI HERB WORKED QUICKLY. LAXMANA SAT UP AND EVERYONE WAS HAPPY.

BUT NOW RAVANA'S BROTHER KUMBHA-KARNA STARTED PLAYING HAVOC ON THE MONKEY ARMY.

HOWEVER, RAMA WAS MORE THAN A MATCH FOR HIM.

AND SOON KUMBHAKARNA FELL.

RAVANA'S SON MEGHNAD WAS KILLED BY LAXMANA.

THE DEMONS WERE NOW ON THE RUN.

IN RAVANA'S CAMP-
HAVE THEY KILLED MEGHNAD?

DETERMINED TO KILL RAMA, RAVANA FOUGHT HARD.

HE SHOWERED A CONTINUOUS STREAM OF ARROWS WITH HIS TWENTY HANDS ON THE MONKEY ARMY.

LAXMANA! MURDERER OF MY SON! YOU WILL NOT LIVE!
THEN RAMA AND RAVANA CAME FACE TO FACE. NOW RAMA HAD A CHARIOT SENT TO HIM BY GOD INDRA.
YOU CAN'T FIGHT RAVANA AND LIVE! THIS BORROWED CHARIOT WILL NOT SAVE YOU!

WITH HIS SUPERNATURAL POWERS, RAVANA CREATED SEVERAL RAVANAS.

THERE WAS PANIC IN THE MONKEY ARMY. ONLY HANUMAN FOUGHT ON BRAVELY.

RAVANA SEEMED UNCONQUERABLE. THOUGH RAMA CUT OFF HIS HEAD SEVERAL TIMES...

...ANOTHER TOOK ITS PLACE AS SOON AS ONE HEAD ROLLED OFF.

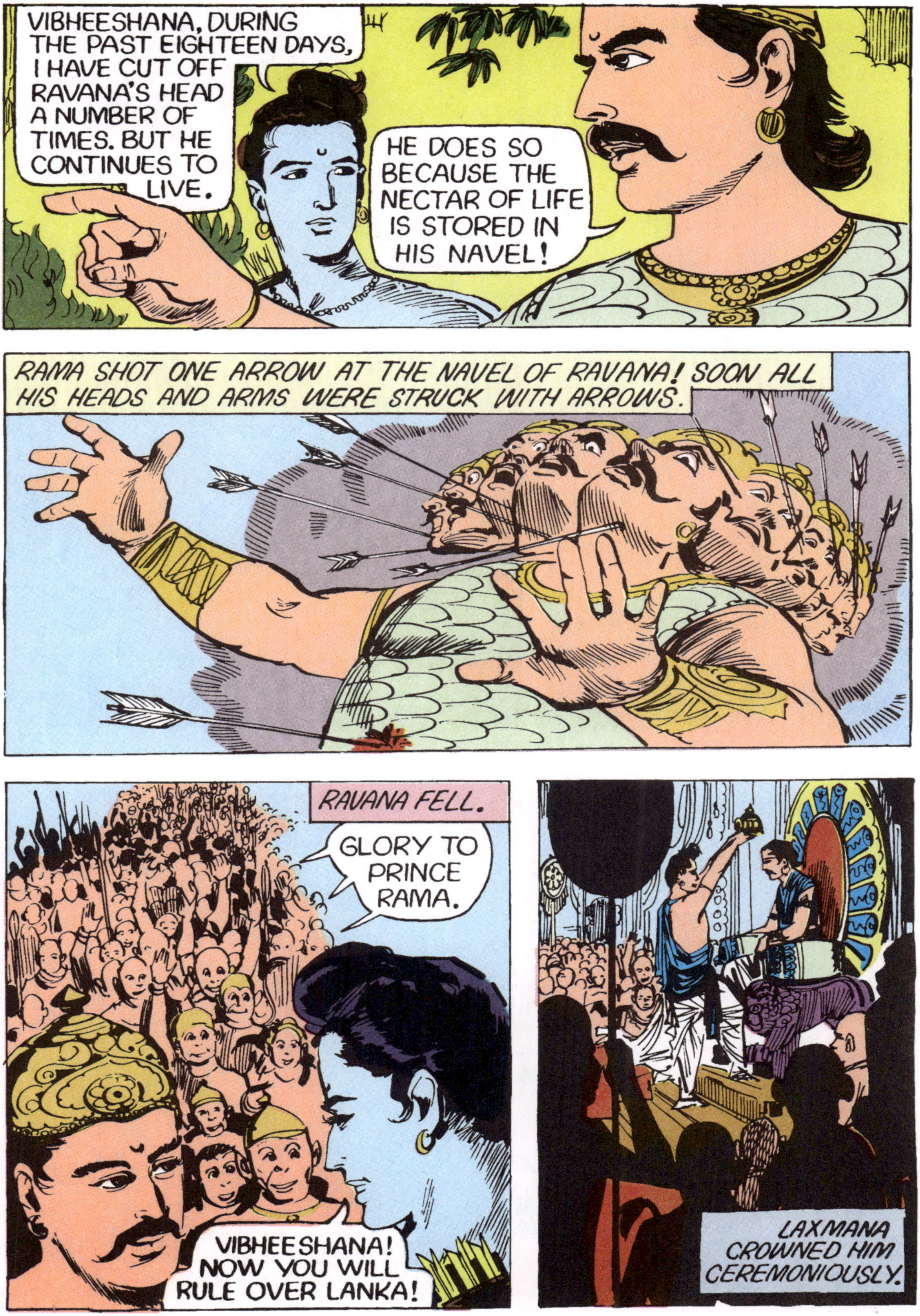
VIBHEESHANA, DURING THE PAST EIGHTEEN DAYS, I HAVE CUT OFF RAVANA'S HEAD A NUMBER OF TIMES. BUT HE CONTINUES TO LIVE.
HE DOES SO BECAUSE THE NECTAR OF LIFE IS STORED IN HIS NAVEL!
RAMA SHOT ONE ARROW AT THE NAVEL OF RAVANA! SOON ALL HIS HEADS AND ARMS WERE STRUCK WITH ARROWS.
RAVANA FELL.
GLORY TO PRINCE RAMA.
VIBHEESHANA! NOW YOU WILL RULE OVER LANKA!
LAXMANA CROWNED HIM CEREMONIOUSLY.

AFTER CROWNING VIBHEE-SHANA, RAMA LEFT FOR AYODHYA IN THE PUSHPAK AIRCRAFT.

SITA, MY DEAR, YOUR DAYS OF UNHAPPI-NESS ARE NOW OVER!

RAMA WAS CROWNED KING IN AYODHYA AND HE RULED FOR MANY YEARS.